I Kiss You Blue

By
Kiana Kleemm

First Edition: February 2019
Printed in India

ISBN: 978-93-87269-89-7

Cover Design & Illustrations: Kiana Kleemm

STORYMIRROR
Stories that reflect you

Publisher:	StoryMirror Infotech Pvt. Ltd. 145, First Floor, Powai Plaza, Hiranandani Gardens, Powai, Mumbai- 400076, India
Web:	www.storymirror.com
Facebook:	www.facebook.com/storymirror
Twitter:	https://twitter.com/story_mirror
Instagram:	https://instagram.com/storymirror

FOREWORD

I am happy to introduce this poetry book 'I Kiss You Blue' by Kiana Kleemm. I have been familiar with Kiana's meticulously written screenplays for shorts and features. I was pleased when Kiana mentioned that she has decided to publish a collection of her poems. Especially because she has a flair for engaging and eloquent visual writing which is evident in her screenplays. Similar evocativeness is apparent in her poems which could paint a picture in the mind of the reader.

Her Poetry truly brings the essence of her empathetic, sensitive yet brave soul. Some of her poems touch our heart, and some make us think about the world we live in whereas, some unveil our sensual self and some confront our deep-rooted pains. Her writing style and range is indeed exhilarating.

'I Kiss You Blue' is an impressive collection of poems which gives profound insight into human experiences. I wish Kiana all the best for her journey as a writer and a creative individual.

Paresh Rawal
(Actor, Dramatist, Producer, MP)

"Like stabs of lightning in a pitch black sky, Kiana Kleemm's flashing words illuminate the vast, secret landscape of the heart and shake our souls awake with fierce passion and childlike joy. At once innocent and knowing, hopeful and heart-rending, this collection of poems is a life-affirming celebration of both the human spirit and the liberating fires of imagination."

_____*Leo O'Sullivan (Screenplay Writer, Script Doctor, Former Script Consultant for Al Pacino, Michael Mann- Heat, Collateral, The Insider and Andrew Niccol- The Truman Show, Gattaca, Lord of War; NY/LA)*

"With Kiana's words you somehow know she is not just speaking to a God or sending a message for guidance. It runs deeper where there is a longing for something lost. A love that is so intense that lives in the essence of her and defines how she navigates the world and the beauty, pain and wonder she shows. Kiana has opened up a part of the soul that not many can do and this debut collection is a great advert for the adventure of life"

___*George Lamptey (Actor/Poet, London)*

"Bold yet layered on diverse impacting ideas. Positively colorful Poetry".

___*Chadwick Struck (Producer/CD, Los Angeles)*

"Kiana Kleemm presents the reader with a delightful rainbow kaleidoscope of poetry, each with it's own unique tone and mood, she examines life's great mysteries; love, ambition, doubt, conflict, family and death. Each poem is a deeply personal take on subjects that each of us consider, a treasure of sensitive and delicate observations, rich with enchantment, magic, cheer, laughter, and joy."

___*Peter Banning(English Literature Professor, Australia)*

"When I read Kiana's poetic writing, I am gently transported into an elsewhere that enchants and delights. She captures a wayward thought and expresses it with taste and exuberance."

___*Arthur W Lake (Togwells Publishing, UK,Canada)*

"Kiana's poems will speak directly to many. They offer a voice for what is often difficult to express."
___***Julie Tharp (Professor,University of Wisconsin)***

"Poetry is like our whisper to nature's ears. Its language of inner soul and sentiments. Kiana's poems have blazing flames of burning volcano and abyss of deep blue sea together. She has art of turning experiences to expressions and expression to a fresh experience for a reader. He poems has blossom of youth, ecstasy of desire, cry of sorrow and joy of being. Her words emotionally capture darkness came from humid mountain cave and sunshine breeze of first rain at the same time. As a woman who has journeyed on her own, she has sensitive perspective for art and life. Passion and pain, pleasure and peace – all one can find in her creations. As an author of my language I welcome this talent to global galaxy of creators. Keep sparkling and soaring high Kiana!"
___***Jay Vasavada (Author, Speaker,Traveler & Lifelover)***

"Eloquent, passionate, breezy yet audacious poetry. A penetrating observation about human behavior and psyche!"
___***S. Prajapati (Filmmaker, NZ)***

"WONDERFUL PRISM OF EXPRESSIVE COLOURS
Kiana's poetry, each in a different mood and class, passes through the prism of thought processes as an individual idea and beautifully brings out the 7 elements and colors of integrity, intimacy, absolute honesty, objectivity, vivid visual expressions, rhythmic crescendos and above all, the exploration of inner self and the universe. Fantastic work! Keep exploring Kiana's work."
___***Dakshesh Pathak (Sr. Journalist, Gujarat Samachar)***

"Some truths are best conveyed by poetry which has often been forgotten as a source of wisdom through the ages. Kiana has captured truths that cannot easily be expressed any other way".
___***William Lake (Author; Ontario, Canada)***

Dedicated to GOD

I know not how to deal with you.
To thank you or to be mad at you.

Without the intricacies of the life that you designed;
These words wouldn't have flowed through my
abducted mind.

In spite of my lost thoughts on you,
I owe it all to you.

After all,
I know that young girl;
All she wanted was a 'Meeting' with you!

Now P.T.O for some kick-ass dedications...

Dedicated to

Ram and Sita,

With all the respect from my heart; Thanks for showing that what kind of man one shouldn't marry and what kind of woman one should never be? It's about him-letting her go, and her-not speaking up, respectively. Love them otherwise!

Dedicated to

My naive, little crazy, sensitive yet strong muscle pumping blood in my body; That one stubborn piece of God's delicately messed up work, barely size of my fist, Still believing in the goodness of humankind,

Making me see beauty in all forms as well as inspiring some uplifting work.

Oh yeah, I wouldn't forget you, 'you grey monster'!

Dedicated to

That mass of 'grey matter' stuck in my skull,

So wonderfully, it works! Generally, I'm happy with it, even proud of it... But Goddamn it! It sometimes forgets to manufacture certain happy chemicals- making me feel much. But this is where the light gets in they say and brings out creativity!

Dedicated to

Meet Joe Black- a movie, where 'Death falls in Love'!

This movie brings two of my favorite subjects- 'Love and Death' together and turns my head because I just love the way 'Death falls in Love' and everything about it!

And lastly,

Dedicated to

Michelle and Barack Obama,

If there were still kingdoms, you both showed how a king and a queen would rule it together. You showed how power is beautifully balanced with kindness and grace by such a lovely union of a man and a woman. You guys are a hell of a solid team..! Nothing can beat you if you are strong at this unit! Thanks for setting an example of that. What I see here also inspired some of my work — lots of love to you both.

ACKNOWLEDGMENT

I take this opportunity to thank some wonderful people in this journey of publishing my book.

I extend my immense thanks to Mr. Paresh Rawal for his ever encouraging support. His name doesn't need an introduction. His humility and kindness are remarkable. I feel grateful to have his honest and impartial feedback on my work. And I was genuinely humbled when he agreed to write the foreword for my book. Thank you, Sir.

I thank the whole team of StoryMirror, for their understanding throughout the process. I like to thank friends and family for their support. I want to thank dearest Bhoomi, especially for being patient to hear me talking about books and publishing even though it's not her domain. Also, thanks to all those souls residing at certain vibrations; for inspiring poems like 'Divine Justice,' 'Filthy Soul' and 'It's Green' and reminding us constantly that we live in Kalyuga!

I want to acknowledge the work of an actor Jodie Foster which has touched me deeply. Whether it's 'Panic Room' or 'Contact' or 'Silence of Lambs'; it has profoundly inspired me in my creative works including poetry. Thank you indeed for creating such work.

I pay sincere gratitude to all the poets who have come before me and have enriched the world of words. Thanks to all those readers and poetry lovers out there, who cherish words. Last but not least; I thank life and its experiences. Because, whenever I dip the brush of my imagination into those, I can always paint the picture with words.

To ever Imagining, ever Writing and ever Creating...!

Cheers!
Kiana

INTRODUCTION

Do you feel you have an unexpressed volcano of emotions that might erupt anytime?
Do you sometimes wonder “Am I the only one feeling this way”?
Do you love to get lost somewhere and still be present?
Do you sometimes think whether you are naive to believe in ‘soul-some’ love?

As you travel through pages of this book, you may find your voice somewhere. You may discover a thought or words which may be a silent catharsis for you.

My journey of poetry started among medicines and prescriptions in London. But it has taken me far from it; towards a true path, never looking back. On this path, I am pleased to share my ‘being’ with you through my poetry.

I believe words give shapes to our being and feelings; and sometimes to our pains. Here in this book, I have opened my soul and lay it bare before you. So, do take care as you hold it in your hands.

Love and Courage,
Kiana

Let's Begin

Inspired by the photo of warrior Queen Boudicca at Westminster Bridge, London. (Near London Eye)

1

WARRIOR

A fiery warrior,
With a calm exterior!

Is that a peaceful warrior?

Sure,
A poet warrior!

I INVOKE YOU

Your rival is coming closer as you pass by.

Dear life,
I command you to come to me and
Fill my breasts with springtime.

Love and joy and pleasures of all kinds;
I invoke you Life,
To come to me in abound!

DELICIOUS KISS

I see the clear blue sky,
In your clear blue eyes.

I want to borrow the rainbow,
From that blue, blue sky;
To smear it in your smile.

Colors of the rainbow, now on your lips;
How Delicious would be that Kiss!

VICTORY

I want a victory of a thousand swords,
Blood dripping bodies and undefeated souls!

Since the times have changed;
I can settle with thousand words.

Success, a form of victory;
It's the best revenge, they say!

You take care of it, God.
Because I want my victory to be filled with joy,
Not revenge!

So, You take care of it!

A thousand words or a thousand swords!
Sometimes words and sometimes swords!

5

THE SIN

Sins of flesh they talk about.
Desires burning, making it all numb.

This numbness pains now;
So, find me sins of soul somehow!

I MISS 'ME'

I still miss,
The times we missed.
The moments we don't share,
The talks we don't talk.
The smiles we don't savor.

Yeah, I still miss;
The kisses in which we don't melt.

Yeah, I miss 'me';
That 'me' I was with you.

READING AND WATCHING A 'DEATH'

It is said, 'power of words' is higher;
But recently I doubted it slighter!

Every great animation, written first on paper!
They started making movies of it,
Well, I don't mind the taste of it!

But, 'Hold' my heart said,
'Watching' Anna die felt stronger than
'Reading' Anna dead!

All she did was to 'fall in love,'
She paid higher than her man of love!

That was and is the society's taste,
Making guilty who are pure innate!

With all due respect dear Tolstoy,
Why be such a fool?
To give her death so foul...!

8

BETWEEN A MAN AND A WOMAN

As your lips venture on the curves of my naked breast;
I feel my lips apart trembling at its best!

Caresses of your fingers, so soft;
Making a layer of me melt, afloat!
And I want more, my heart yearns!

Your hands, traveling and exploring,
Every inch of my skin.
I feel ecstasy as you travel far,
You rise and enter, 'what a bliss' I cry!

You explore me, being in me;
And I let you, feeling in me!
Moments of sighs from me and you,
You hold me so tight like I'm a part of you.

Intertwined our thighs; we touch, and we sigh!
After a moment of exhaustion, there you lie;
On my naked breast, like a naughty child.

I caress your hair so soft, and plant a kiss so gentle;
You equally kiss on my temple.

You pull me much closer, and hold me so tight;
I love your 'hold,' on my naked soul and my thighs.

In that embrace;
I feel at peace and safe by your side.
And I sleep like a baby under your hide.

I want this moment to last forever,
So I clench my fist, kiss and release it to the universe!

How beautiful it would be;
You protect and provide, I nourish and nurture!
Aligning the unspoken promise;
Between a man and a woman!!!

THE CHARADE

Dear World,
If you kill my innocence,
I will be fit to live in the opulence.

But,
When that charade ends;
There will be blood on your hands!

SOMETHING AMISS

You have everything.
Accolades, riches and many pretty things.

Yet,
You're missing out on something.
Someone reaching out to you,
Enriching that everything.

Yes,
You are 'someone' and 'somebody' in the world.

Yet,
Not a 'world' to 'someone',
Whose world would stop without your presence!

Yes, you have everything.
But, Something amiss.

Because you don't have me.

So, watch out and feel the air around,
When I reach out to you,
To find my world in you.

11

***FINALLY...! ***

Over Sensitive I am;
I've been told many times.

But loneliness in crowds;
Never understood by any kind.
I only think and the phone rings;
Thought I was a telepath.

Someone's sad eyes; And my heart aches.

I finally discovered;
I am an Empath….!!

At last a relief, an awakening;
Many answers and a knowing.

Those pains felt;
Were not mine…
I am just fine…!

I felt,
Because
I am an Empath….!!!

YOU FELL IN LOVE

When you read me,
You fell in love.

You fell in love with love and with my words.

I knew!
So, I smiled.

I held my breath,
To catch your breath.

Because I knew;
That you fell in Love with me,
When you read me.

TO HOLD & TO HAVE

Your look would be a catharsis,
On my soul and my spirit.

And you would know something,
That a Queen would ask for nothing.
The Queen only demands.

Yet,
For that look of yours,
Piercing through my soul,
Through the crowded shores.
I break my rule and can even ask.

But a kind reminder to only a king;
If a queen asks,
She would ask for nothing less than a kingdom!

Go and find that;
And I promise myself to you,
To Hold and to Have.

LOVE YOU
WE LOVE YOU TOGETHER
VICTORY YES
VICTORY TO U BOTH

POWER IN YOUR HANDS

I see 'you' smile,
So humble and shy.

I see 'me,'
Watching you from afar.

Help me God, for what I say!
'Power' would be so good in your hands.

Oh why? You ask.

Since you carry a sound head,
And a kind soul too, in your heart.

DOUBLE DEATH

And we just did the deed.
To seal the deal,
We thought of some cake to lick.

The delicious chocolate cake called,
Coco Death.

We ate some,
Missed some,
Spread some, on parts of ours some.

On his lips, Traces of Coco death.
I licked,
That last bit of coco death.

His lips and breath and the evil mess of coco death.
Hmmm,
I wouldn't have minded 'Double Death'!

***HUMAN SPIRIT ***

They stood there.
Then they were ordered to crouch.

They obeyed.
Who killed whom thousands of years ago?
Who paid for whose sins, how do we know!

Fascinates me, the courage of the human spirit;
Bread was shared - even the little crumbs.

Bodies;
Insulted, crushed, stripped and gassed.
But the souls survived those goddamn camps!

A GIFT

Clothes are never to be ordered from the net;
Sizes are different, so the hips and waist.

I just took a chance of ordering some,
Keeping a doubt in mind of returning some.

But to my surprise, it arrived quite well.
I recall the happy moment of that day;
A gift-wrapped parcel and my heart was all gay.

It's always a joy opening a gift;
Doesn't matter the person gifting me was 'me.'

18

YOU BETTER BE THERE

I hear your footsteps in the air,
Very handsome is your gait.

At the gate of my fate, I eagerly await.
Footsteps coming closer and closer,

My heart waits for its abductor.
I close my eyes, holding my breath!

But when I turn around,
You better be there!

WITHOUT A NAME

Throbbing or mild,
Piercing or numb,
Sharp or dull;
Are the types of known pain.

Yet,
There are some pains,
Without any names...!

IT BROKE LOOSE

Her moistened lips and parts,
Her brightened eyes.

A genteel man on a gallant horse;
With his intoxicated smile.

Eyes met;
Spirits lifted.

More, the moistened lips part;
The garter then, torn apart.

Enclosed in each other,
They let it loose.

And just then,
All 'heaven' broke loose!

21

I DECIDE

For a long while,
I've tried to evade your gift.

Seeing unseen;
Knowing unknown;
Understanding untold.

To get close to you,
You test us, they say!
You give us a gift to bear.

Yes,
I tried to evade bearing your gift.
I searched for camouflages that sit.

But your gift full of courage,
Always shone through!

So now,
I realize something and with much joy,
I decide to bear.

I understand,
You had given me;
'My cross to bear'...!

LITTLE JOYS

My favorite buy, halogen oven;
Not so big as a conventional oven.

Little joys came from having it,
Using to bake a cake, pizza, and many things.

Fancy dress, shoes, and many expensive means;
But this modest buy brings a smile to my lips.

I like the feeling of having it;
Knowing joy can come from little things!

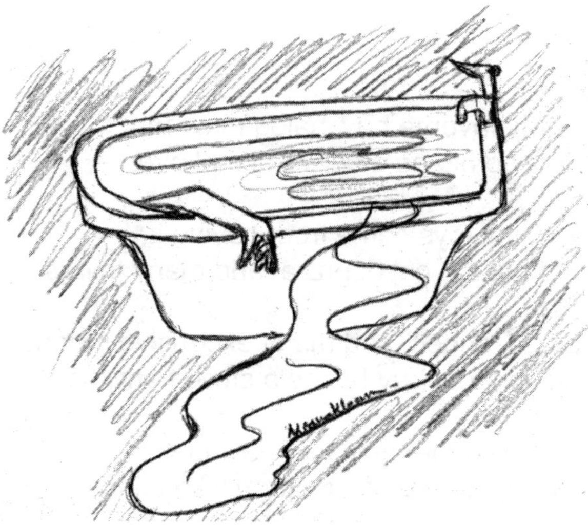

POOL OF BLOOD

She drowned in the pool of the blood.
Blood of pain and suffering,
Oh yeah, and a lot of doing!

Yes,
She drowned in that pool of blood.
But the blood was not hers.

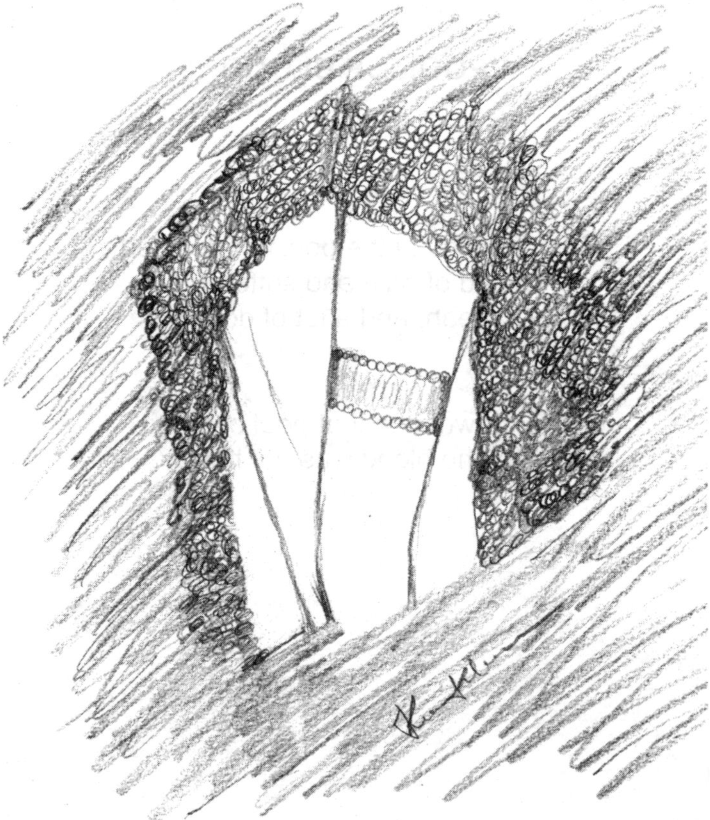

I HID IT

In the saddest of all places,
I hide my Joy!

I hid it in myself,
The pain felt at the pleasant spot.

A DROPLET

You are like a huge wave rushing,
Full of vigor, hustling.

I wish not to be the sand on a sunny beach,
Where you would come and go in a breeze.

I would rather be a 'droplet',
Hidden inside you.

So that,
Without the multitudes of 'me',
You wouldn't be 'you'.

I LOVE DEATH

I love death,
It's clear and clean.

Life has its prerogatives- drama and desires.

Death is simple.
It acts without any tantrums!

Life is different to different kinds,
But my sweet death is fair to all kinds.

It simply comes and takes, never discriminates!

So dear death,
Since I hold you in such high regard,
Would you please give me a little notice,
Just before you arrive?!

CONSUMPTION

You consume me,
Mind, Body and Spirit.

Pieces of me, lying next to you;
Yet,
I never felt so whole before you.

If that's how I reach divinity,
Then I want to be consumed by you,
For eternity.

THEN LIFE HAPPENED..!

Alright, I prayed for long;
Many times for others and also for the world.
A selfless yet tortured soul. Why?

Then, life happened.
I learned to pray for myself.

And I realized;
You listen yet not reply,
You watch yet not see,
You show me the way yet not guide the way,
You show me 'fire' in me yet not provide me wood,
You sense me yet not acknowledge,
You make me desire yet not align the stars,
You see my toil, and you grin yet not smile!

Dear God,
Why this negligence?

Frankly,
I prefer two-way communication!

MEMORIES

As I try to sleep, closing my eyes;
Your memories surround my mind.

A piece of my heart,
Gone away with you.

Yet,
It gives a peace to my heart,
When your memories surround my mind.

30

IT'S GREEN

Its color is green.
It kills with a glance so mean.

And when you catch 'it' in the eye;
It turns in despise.
It gathers the weak minds;
To make you feel apart.
It conspires!

It hurts you with an evil eye.
It's ignited in those minds,
By you just 'being you.'
It turns ugly when it rises.
It curses you bad when it flares.
I know, it causes pain!

Even then,
Be Okay. Be You.
You don't need to please those minds.
Oh! It will infuriate those kinds;
Since those are insecure minds!

How much dumb can you play?
Just rise above, and Be You.

And that,
'It' will stay below you.

Didn't you recognize 'it'?
That 'green', that 'it' is Envy.
When you make it stay below you;
That green 'Envy' will stay away from you.

UNBORN

They say you take us through a tunnel,
Some even say through a white door!

I'd wondered since my tender age;
Where would you take me after this cage?

Well, I do have some choices,
Or perhaps preferences!
About where to be born and where not to be born.

Can we make a deal my sweet death?
Because I'd rather stay 'Unborn'!

CHAMPAGNE SOCIALIST

Clever minds, wearing masks!
They say it's all the same in the society we exist!!

Is it the same? Or will it ever be?
Hold on a second, my agile heart screams.

"Why Should it be?"
Those clever people argue!

After all,
We are very fine, and they are thick.
Let them be just that and keep them the same;
So that,
We can sit from where we can see their game!

I was disturbed, and I left my seat.
After all,
I am not a champagne socialist!

NEON
EFFECT

NEON IS FLASHING

Neon is flashing,
And I don't see the light!

Am I really blind or
You're not yet in my sight?!

IN GOD WE TRUST
LIBERTY
1879

IN GOD WE TRUST

(Behind a Quarter Dollar)

I know you are there;
Up there, somewhere!

Busy with pulling strings,
Of the puppets of the stage called 'World'!

But, listen!
Don't pull my strings so much.

If you do;
I will always have faith in you,
But 'trusting you' would be painful!

I don't see you yet I believe in you.

That's the proof,
How much I should mean to you!

BE CAREFUL...!

In your artistry, I trust my destiny;
In your joys, I hide my sorrows;
In your life, I hide my death;
In your spirit, I hide my soul.

Be careful,
How you carry yourself;
Because at every step,
You carry ‘me’ too with yourself…!

PIANO VIRGIN

Ahhhh! What an evening it was;
Music, enveloping my heart and soul.

The dainty hands played the piano;
A touch so smooth, arms up and down with care.
The music truly consuming the hall;
No wonder people in old times fell in love at the ball..!

The aesthetically pleasing music it was to ears;
But watching the pianist was also inspiring to my vision!

Taking the breath and stretching her back;
Then a swift thrust forward; traces covering her neck.

The caresses on piano, of the fingers so soft;
Producing the music, rather so strong!
A little move forward and a little backward she made;
But what an elegant form, she played all well!

The greatest composers were little crazy,
The ecstasy of music is very compelling!

Oh God, I urge thee,
Provide me with the means of learning;
I surely don't want to die 'Piano Virgin'!

37

FILTHY SOUL

Dear Narcissist,
You think you're unseen?

I see you.
I see through your pitiful soul!

Whenever we regain our center,
We see your games.
Games you cleverly played...!

You have a strategy, pretty full proof!
Carefully you choose your victims;
Then move stealthily on their vulnerabilities.

You put people on a pedestal.
Then at their happiest,
You kick the bottom…!
Throwing them on the floor,
Scattered...!

This drama gives you a 'kick',
That you've power over 'How others feel'...!
Then you make them doubt themselves!

Your victims;
Sucked dry and drained;
Now, nothing is left for you to take.

They lose their center!
And just then you show your true demeanor-
'Narcissistic disposal'...!

Smoothly you move on to your next victim;
Showing all your grandeur!

On and on, on this game;
You will always be less of a man!

I pity you,
You filthy soul!

A ROSEBUD

Scattered flowers;
On the high street.

The crowd went by,
In boots and high heels.

In a rush, I was;
Yet, I managed to stop.

Oh!
I bent down in no know;
And up with a 'rosebud'.

Tiny bud and dainty stem,
I put it in the water, when I took it home,

And,
I wait for a hidden Rose;
Within that 'Rosebud.'

PARALYZED LOVE

Some bonds are just weak,
Soul screams from the peak.

This facade of love;
Most misunderstood and bespoke!

Love would standby, and it'd make you strong;
'Never ever lose heart', it'd shout from the roof.

If that's not the case, in 'your case';
It's a 'Paralyzed Love' my friend!

*** CERTAINTY***

Certainty,
A kind of rarity!

Only the fortunate one experiences,
The solid certainty about something.

It may come once in a lifetime,
But it can make your life springtime!

DIVINE JUSTICE

A bully. A coward. Sitting across the table.
Using harsh words at me, to make himself look big.

These kinds of people, steal others' wind;
To fill the sails of their ship.

If a curse can come true;
Then I do, I do curse him who drained my soul.

For tonight,
I allow my nightmares to creep in my sleep.
But to you;
Who think you are all fair,
Raising your voice in all your flair.
Your well-calculated humiliation and twisted words;
What a damn master manipulator you were.

I know not of these fancy plays,
But let me say;
A game that you played,
By someone else, you will be played.

‘Forgiveness’ they teach in the church,
‘Letting go’ in temples.

‘Revenge’ I agree is not good for the soul;
But will you take care of it, my lord?

Will you show your Divine Justice and
Raise me above these games, dear God!

42

THE ROAR AND THE CALM

Some hearts just pump blood,
Some fiercely beat!

I thought,
What's the point of blood in those veins, running;
If it doesn't boil and rush at the summoning!

Heart pounds at the roaring ocean;
Yet,
Craves the comfort of a serene lake.

Show me the balance in my being,
The roar and the calm in the same feeling.

FAMILY LOTTERY

I see you have a father to guide,
I see you have a mother by your side,
On the path,
Which you want to ride.

'Yours' are your strength,
It must be amazing bonds.

Their love is shown by understanding your ride,
Not the type of love which simply frets,
And mess it all up with unnecessary rite!

Love makes one strong, it never hesitates!
Is it love if it weakens and fluctuates?

Siblings to share laughter and sweet fights.

Some do.
Some do have these all, without a notary;
The best gift from universe is a 'Family Lottery'!

THE SKY AND THE EARTH

There was a sky,
And the earth.

Earth waited,
As the sky tried to touch the strongness of the earth.

It seemed to have happened at some point.
At 'zenith'.

But what an illusion..!

Sky never touched the earth
Stayed above,
Always and forever…!

45

WHAT TURNS YOU ON?

What turns you on?
Life or Death,
Pain or Pleasure,
Abysmal dark or blinding light?

Does Life hurt?
Not much and yet very much so.

Would you side a monster or an angel?
What if a monster comes in a guise of an angel?

Don't let your conscience be devoured,
Don't let it be fooled by the jungle around.

And yet,
Some shades of the same world turn me on,
While I ride on life to meet death!

I WANNA TALK DIRTY

Her voluptuous body, Full breasted chest.
Walking like a nymph,
And dancing in a saree so wet!
Oh, she says;
"I've talked normal enough, and now I wanna talk dirty!"

Yup, that was a bloody shock!
After a break so long!
Then some rummaging and what I found!
It is their norm. They call it a 'Item song'.

And I realized,
Long time back, the seed was sawn.
A man made a song asking
"What's behind your blouse?"
I wonder if he has made "What's behind my trousers?"
Guess, not.

Well,
Men earning money off half-naked women dancing!
Isn't there is a word for that kind of work in
every gathering?

CY
CLUB

Those women wonder;
If they didn't dance, someone else might do it.
But the men who are making it, will get it!

So, those beauties, those screen-goddesses;
With their erotic words and dance,
Seduce the youth and all, at large!

Then as the movie releases;
They hammer the bloody song,
Like a strip-club in every living room.
In towns and villages and every corner,
Penetrating the collective subconscious!

The young boys grow up thinking,
This is what women are for.
Most of these men do not have the exposure;
Of the literary discussion Or any other version.

So, what reaches in every corner of the country,
A 'Money-song'!
Filled with lusty loins, erotic innuendo and some thongs.
Do you blame men,having turn-on watching this norm?

Those smart filmmakers, make sure of zooming.
These beauty's well-endowed breasts and cleavage, blossoming!
Navel and belly; shown all in glory!

Nope,
Not a beautiful and sensual 'love-making' scene!
This is a woman dancing and 'making money' scene!

The movie may or may not have much,
But those guys have this 'money-song.'
Their 'wild-card' at least...!

They make sure their 'golden-hens' are safe!
They come and go with guards!

They don't have to take a bus after watching a movie,
They don't have to take a train after the office,
They don't have to take a cab,
after working at a call-center!

They live in some bubble of his;
Where only fewer people live.

Specially in some parts, in collective male minds,
These songs do project,
That the women are objects.
They imprint and cleverly objectify without any shame.
No wonder this country has so many cases of r**e.
Where a half-naked women dancing,
In the name of beautiful craft as acting.

Can you blame those boys to who are served,
Sensuality in only this manner,
Showing women in a certain low fashion.
Not those women to blame, who dance-
There would always be someone to dance.

It's those men who started and make,
'Money-songs' to have their big fucking cake.
The camera goes much low in her cleavage,
How low they can stoop to make leverage!

Of course, not all are to blame.
Some beautiful work and souls to acclaim.
But an only 'bucket of rose-water',
Around stinking sewage running!

If you don't belong to filmy mafia families-
'By blood or by bond';
You instead go and find a pearl in the ocean,
Than steam of rose-water in this stench commotion.

The air is polluted here.
The art seems stained here.

There are different kinds of woods,
A lion rules some woods,
Talent and craft rule some woods.

But until there is an uprise;
Filmy mafia men obscenely rule this wood.
This is called Bollywood.

CHOCOLATE

Chocolate, Chocolate,Chocolate.
How could we resist it slightest?

Vianne opens a little 'chocolatier'.
Rather delicately, it transforms the town.

She makes chocolate with unusual things;
Chilli, pepper, cinnamon, and mint.

Town Mayor who sticks to the book and rules;
In the name of religion and culture, many are so cruel!

There is no civilization without pleasure;
Why don't some get it for now and forever!

Well, the mayor goes into the shop;
To break and destroy it all.

Just a sliver of chocolate goes in his mouth,
Not intentionally but accidentally at last!

And he sobs;
He knows now,
He was wrong...!

With

some

'Choco-Love'

and...

With a Small hiatus..!
Ending here, this harmony.

To start another Journey.......

I KISS YOU BLUE

I steal the Blue from that
Blue Blue sky!
I mix that Blue with 'something blue'
I wear at the altar.

As I claim you from God;
Looking deep into your Blue Blue eyes;
I take vows.

I take vows that;
With this ring so true,
For now and ever,
I Kiss You Blue!

Kiana is a poet, actor, optioned screenwriter and an empath.
A Free spirit,
Yet yearning to be bound only by love and kindness!

Kiana thrives on the energy while writing and creating art, whether it is poetry, screenplay or performance. She has been an avid reader since very young age.

'I Kiss you Blue' presents the essence of her understanding of life, experiences, pain, pleasures, love, beauty and sorrows.

While reading Kiana's Poems, you will experience those 'Little Joys' of daily lives as well as deep dive into human psyche where you feel you rather stay 'Unborn'!

To know more about her work and see her performance,
Please visit ***www.kianakleemm.com***

Facebook: kianakleemm
Instagram @kianakleemm
Contact:kianakleemm@gmail.com

Other #SMBooks

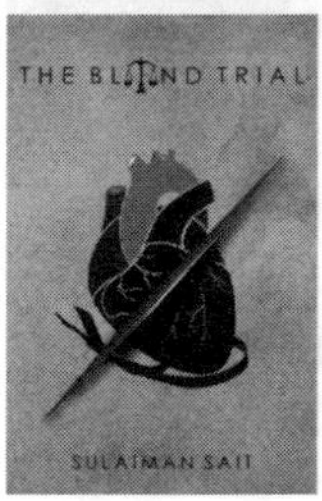

Other #SMBooks

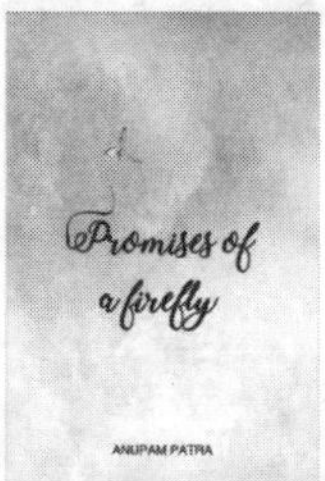